Closeness without fear,

Distance without guilt

Human poems

AF205164

Ann Malone

Closeness without fear,
Distance without guilt

Human poems

Ann Malone

Bibliografische Information der Deutschen Nationalbibliothek: Die Deutsche Nationalbibliothek verzeichnet diese Publikation in der Deutschen Nationalbibliografie; detaillierte bibliografische Daten sind im Internet über dnb.dnb.de abrufbar.

Closeness without fear, distance without guilt

Human poems

Cover Ann Malone

Printed and publishing: BoD-Books on Demand, Norderstedt.

These poems are based on my experience as a human on this earth and my interaction with the human race. Any resemblance to actual people living or dead (besides myself), events or locales on this or other planets is entirely coincidental.

ISBN: 9783748150794

Acknowledgements

Thank you to my family and friends who have accompanied me through my life no matter what the weather.

Thank you to my husband Rolf and my girls, Molly and Emma for their constant supply of love, support, inspiration and understanding in my life.

Thank you to all my pals, you know who you are. You have kept me sane and kept me laughing and listened to me moaning without complaint.

This book is dedicated to us all, human, vulnerable, searching for love and understanding. Sometimes we get lost along the way but our nearest and dearest don't give up on us and pull us out of the deep dark depths and let us shine again.

Hear me

All the babies of the world
Crying out for love and recognition
Some of them now dressed in
Suits and fancy frocks
Lined faces or polished exteriors.

Green

You ache thinking you had it bad
Thinking if only
If only you had what I had
And I ache equally sad
Wishing that I had what you had
Relieved of the burdens I carry
Relieved of what makes me mad.

Moonlight

The quivering shadows glide through the moonlit
forest
I edge my way though the depth of crisp autumn
leaves
No rich colours can be seen
Just the pale glimmer of light peering through the trees
The icy wind cuts bitterly through the scurrying
creatures.

Heartbeat

I listen to your heartbeat
As I hold you close
I could listen to that
For ever
The gentle patter
The sound I love most.

A lifetime of heartbeats
Our private reserve

What about those
Wasted on worry
On anger
On swallowed feelings
On things for which
We don't care.

Let's use up our heartbeats
Now
Dancing
Laughing
Crying
Singing
Screaming
Vibrating together.

Summer

Mossy pillows through which the seeping water's edge
Contrasting with the rushing torrents cascading into a
Deep plunge pool of foaming upheaval
The towering trees with arms of gentle pine and
Sweet heavy scents lower themselves to mingle
With the bright green of the rich undergrowth
Hilarious laughter and screeching hysterically
Drowned maidens race in frenzy, breaking
The calmness of the valley but blending
In the joy of summer.

Indepth

Seeping thoughts not thoroughly eager
Contemptuous grievance strong yet meagre
Could you attempt it all strength combined
Logic and desperation confronting aligned

Is it just an evil passing thought?
Will it return and burn like frost?
Are you sane for anything?
Are you pondering on how things have been?

Even your heart doesn't matter anymore
It overflowed and dried to the core
Simplicity it is with nobody in mind
Confusing it is with thoughts of this kind

A windswept day, forgotten dreams
A complete person ripped at the seams
A windswept day, nothing is clear
All inside is fatigue and fear.

Stripped

The bitter wind armed with spears of ice
Strips the trees bare
Their arms rise up in woe
The destructor whistles on by
Without a care.

Off she goes

This time down the chute
To that other level
But I know now
There's light above
Why do I let myself
Sink again with such regularity.

Chance

I was given a chance
I took it and ran
It wasn't so bad but
I needed the change

Chances to change are everyday
But crises force the issue
Reach out of the steady flow
Seems impossible till the flow stops

A helping hand, a bridging leap
May ease the speed to surface
This chance to step, though often there
Is missed without conscious effort

It's hard to feel loved
If you don't think it's possible
The walls so high
Cannot be just broken

Take down the bricks one by one
Look at them and discard
If you pick the right ones
You'll be surprised to see your walls crumble.

Scrap heap

Back on the scrap heap again
Struggling with thoughts of hope and disillusion
Another start, another chance,
Another
Kick in the ass.

I didn't even feel comfortable
With the whole idea of the job
But I got comfortable
Got to know people
Learned new things
A new world opened

Now, I'm hurled into space again
No limits
No barriers
Freedom
Heaven or hell

Responsibilities hanging on me
Family mouths to feed
Trust it will work itself out
Just let it be

It is as it is.

Closed

Risks, I take them
The bigger the better
The small ones remain
The real ones that matter

Risk, letting you go
Letting you in
Feeling my fears
The risks from within

Hurt I have known
It's hiding down there
Disguised but upset
You think I don't care

I could have told you
If I'd only realized
Confirm what you'd thought
What you'd seen in my eyes.

Fireworks concealed

You touched me not realizing
I'd transformed to a human firework
Biochemical madness exploding in my veins
Tingling and glowing in a crowded room.

It doesn't take much
A twinkling smile, a nod,
An understanding
Oxytocin soaring,
Dopamine disappearing
So it can't be blamed
For instinctual lust.

Awake

The cock crows three times
And I awake to feel and see
The new morning
The clear sky
The new beginnings
Crawl out of the quagmire of thought
Surface from beneath the load
Realise today is fresh
Seeds of thought
Ready to grow.

Needs

He was once young
With cut knees and tears
He will be old
With his aches and fears
In between he will
Seek to be loved
To have someone think him great
He may wander the world
Or stay in one place
Religion, race or colour
Is all the same
When you're hungry
Your body aches
Your heart pains.

Unsure

Hovering above the surface
Touching none.

Time

Tick tock, Tick tock
I can't feel it now
Its slipping by
Minute and hour

Tick tock, Tick tock
It's pulsing through my veins
Every second is critical
And I'll be late again.

Strings

Home is where the heart is
And my heart is divided
My love equally strong
In so many places
Pulled strings in every direction
Roots put down and pulled up
Sprouts shot out in every direction
Peace in my heart, in my soul
Only when I realise
I am at home in myself
Bathed in love.

Business

He smells of boardroom
As he scurries along
One meeting to another
The pressure of decisions
Bearing on his neck.

His defensive shell ready
His tumbling stomach
His intellect searching crevices
For words to be said.

He will speak
Their reaction will be grave
He has seen it before
Somehow it doesn't
Touch him anymore
Anticipation and impatience
As he finds his place
In Command.

Old

Her face tell so many stories
And still I fail to see
Her as a young girl skipping along to school
Only when she laughs
And her eyes glimmer in a dreamy way
Can I catch a glimpse
Of that life that once was.

Move it

Step in
Step out
Step in
Step out
Ad infinitum

A never ending loop
A continuous circle
And there in the centre
Is me
Dizzy

Yes, No
Break, go
Yes, no
What is it?

Take a step out
Regardless of the consequences
Security is one thing
Frozen, the alternative
Do it.

Rotting badness

That harmless old woman
Was once feared by all
Not respected with gentleness
Not helped for her frailty
Her sharp words
Her evil deeds
Don't get a chance
With bodily decay.

Divided

He was eager to please
Everyone and thing
But the drag of each way
Pulled him apart
He shattered and scattered
Leaving nothing within
Nothing to know what was
Really him.

Gossip

A word here, a word there
No evil intention at all
But what was it
Nothing else to say
But to ruin people's lives.

Cheat

He listened, he understood
I really felt he cared
He offered support but
It supported his own cause.

A whispered word
A knowing look
A nod, raised eyebrows
The deed was done.

Truth

I believe my thoughts
They are my version
Of the truth
If I question my thoughts
I might find
Another version
Others might react
Differently in
That version
And my reality
May be
Changed.

Free

The sunshine is brighter bursting through the fog
The salt is sharper on a tongue drenched in sweetness
The anger more profound in one used to reserve
The breaking of routine more thrilling
In one used to the mundane.

Tidal

The blue moon rises
Soaking everything
In its path
In the loveliest glow
It pulls the tides
The saps of trees
I'm mostly water
What is it doing
To me?

Split

The relationship split
And the details
Spilt over the white carpet
For all to see
To analyse
To tear further apart
No amount of
Band-aid
Will ever
Close that rift
Not even heavy duty
Sticking tape
Could bring those
Damage parts
Together again.

Peace

The wood pigeon called me back
To my swaying swing in the garden
Where I felt so well
There the dew grass soaked my shoes
And slowly seeped in to greet my toes
Where the sun shone and the morning quiet
Stayed with me a lifetime to meet me
Here again, years later, in the wood.

Hidden?

The curved back
Reveals the story
My mouth conceals

This open mouth
Reveals the story
You choose to believe.

No obstacle

Baby steps will get you up the mountain
Baby steps will get you out of here
Bring you a new life
Free of that fear

The fear of moving in any direction
The feeling that it's all too much
The terror that you're making the wrong decision
The dread you've lost your touch

Lost touch with what is really you
Stuck in a body revolting
Revolting against all it has swallowed
Throwing up all it has held back

Baby steps in a new direction
Any direction is better than none
One foot forward, the other will follow
Today is the day
This is the one.

Choked

The ivy's attached
Growing and choking
Waiting for my collapse

Its hold too strong
For me to break loose
To breathe freely
To nourish my branches

The end is sure
But my end is its as well.

Future

Every fortune teller could tell you
You are going to die
And it would be true
Sometime, maybe in the distant future
But how distant in the lifetime of the planet.

Lost warmth

I cannot hold your embrace
Only in my heart
And in my memory
That too will fade

Only this moment I can
Enjoy, wallow in its warmth
Suck up all its goodness
And glow this moment in happiness.

Acid

Bitterness robs all energy
Gnaws the brain, body, heart
Slipping into oblivion
Till all is numb
Blank
Cold.

Deserted

No medication, no food
The poor are happy?
No roof, not clean
Stinking, nobody comes near

All medication, all food
Money's not everything?
Big villa, big guards
Stinking rich, alone?

Vibration

These sounds you utter
Mean something to you
As I look on clueless
As you chat and laugh
And you change mood
Depending on the sounds
You hear in your ear

To me it is all meaningless
I utter slightly different sounds
Which open up my world
Expanding my experience.

Soiled

Wailing like toddlers
In this valley of tears
Nappies full
Disturbing our stride
No-one to clean up the mess
But ourselves

Rip off those nappies
Clean ourselves off
Toddle on again
Don't let the shit
Build up.

Up to speed

You can't drive
With the brakes full on
Now you're accelerating
With no direction.

Budding

I knew myself as a child
But now the growing's sprung every way
In leaps and bounds, in all directions
That's me,
Trapped in this new body.

My sweetest moments begin
Don't you hear the old me
With the new voice and body
And the new me
You are getting to know.

Me too, with ideas and opinions to match your own
I'm the new adult, I see things clearly
I haven't a huge past, no hindsight
No bitterness or heavy burdens to sway my thoughts.
I'm fresh.
Can't you see me?
Sprouting like a springtime bud
Full of excitement and joy at my new beginning
Full of frustration and nervousness
With the rapid change and newness

Here comes my body,
Growing and changing at a rapid rate
Leaving my baby body behind

The child in me hidden inside.

Care

It's hard to strike a balance
Of our emotional swings each day
And harder still to balance
The delicate difference of caring and worrying

Worrying destroys no matter what
Caring leaves enough energy to use
To build, to grow, to understand
We all do what we have to do.

Mother

Sleep baby sleep
Your mother watch will keep
But as you grow
She's forced to let go

To not know
What will happen to you
As you walk in
This world
Without her.

Sunday - Birth

Just as your mother brought you
You brought me and
I brought Molly out into
The world to see

The sunshine
The showers
Dark forest
Bright flowers
The smiling, the crying
The laughing, the sighing
Thank you.

Monday - Nourish

Shovel it into you
Up to the brim
All gone Mammy
Mash the lumps in

Frustration, delight
Watch her grow
Tomatoes, brown bread, scallions
For once, let her say no

The saucy pops
Cups of cocoa
Ice cream, more and more
Pandy, onions, drop scones
And crusts of bread galore

No more spoon feeding
Now she's started to bake
Just mess everywhere
Under the bed, a cake

Fast food essential
Now she discovered her friends
Coat flying wide open
Where will it all end?

Tuesday - Growth

Shy unassuming
Eager to please
The fairies brought the hormones
Guaranteeing big change

But the essentials are embedded
Truth and honesty to be gained
Appreciation of others differences
Wild temper to be tamed.

Wednesday - Friendship

Hand in hand we walked along
Loving each other's company
Of something we would never tire

Our roles in life keep changing
But our deepest feelings the same
No matter what the differences
Our truest friendship remains

Thursday - Nature

Clontarf was beckoning
Leaves collected and shown
Cows eating in the manger
The path well worn

Fascination by everything living
Eagerness and interest you show
No hectic, but peace and gentleness
Because your pace is slow.

Friday - Emotions

The emotions came frothing
Eager to go
Torn by ups and downs
Highs turning to lows
Your patience awaiting
The bubble ready to burst
I never realized till recently
How closely our emotions entwined
Caring so much for each other
But burdened by each other's lives.

Saturday - fun

The three generations
In the posh surroundings
Baby in the sink,
Polished and gleaming around us
Switzerland this funny link

Laughing and giggling with chiselers
The ridiculous of it all the same
Tickled by the picture of ourselves
Displaced in this world so sane

Years of laughing in the bathroom
Knickers on our heads
Sshh and giggle and shhh again
Your Dad is in the bed.

Show on out the back today
Buns for the tuppenny worth
The party's in the shed today
With money from your purse.

Sunday - circle of life and love

The good night song
Cuddling me near
A mother and back up
For assurance guaranteed

The sacred heart of Jesus
Lived in your heart too
Giving me so much each day
Bringing out the best in you

Your belief that the best would come
Sorted out by the Lord above
The belief that no matter what
He was there to love

We're part of a bigger picture
Something we can't quite comprehend
Something balanced and loving
Something for our start, living and end.

Away

The call came
And even though
I knew it would come
Played the scene in my head
A thousand times

I wasn't ready
I never would be.

My dear Daddy

You saved me from the crocodiles
As I hung around your neck
You cordoned off my bit of garden
Gave me tools from your shed

We raced down the road as you beeped
For a jant on your motorbike
You took us by car to see your ma
On a Saturday night

Stuffed on the goodies
Lemonade up our noses
Tired from the excitement
On the way home we would doze

All squashed in the tiny mini
We headed off to Ashtown
Out to the little pub
Mini scraping the ground

Off to Dollier, Portmarnock
Down to the sea
Summer in the air
Paddling up to our knees

Holidays down in Wexford
Stop for country butter on the way
Out with the primus stove
Boil up the water
For a cup of tae

The years passed quickly
Little girls growing up
You warned us of the dangers
Of the drink and the pub

You told me to take care of myself
My life was my own
But if I ever got into trouble
Never forget to come home,

We've had many's a good laugh
Along life's weary road
Thank you for all your support
It has helped me to grow.

Thank you.

Sleep

Sleep unwinds each nut that's overstrained in the brain
Each aching muscle unfolds like elastic set free
It demands nothing but with it so much is gained
When all doors are closed sleep has the key.

Uplifted

A change of mood, a change of sense
Sprung from a passing word, a smiling face
Tremendous gloom, suppressing thoughts fade.
The softness of moss, sweet scents prevail.

Uplifting from the tension of sinking eyebrows
Doom drawn back, letting brightness flood in.
Surging hilarity from this well, appeared
Eagerly forcing through the swamps of doubt.

Gone

I decided to die
They buried me today
So many people there
No one there when I lived

Nobody cared
Couldn't stand their way
Of going on
Never fit in
Not my roots

Even my roots were rotten
Now I'm in the earth
Looking for new roots
Hoping to have a place
I can have peace and quiet

How can you stand there?
What do you feel?
What is different to when
I stood there?

What are you crying for?
I'm the one who cries
Cry for yourself and
This ridiculous world
I never saw any sense in it all
I'm off now,

Goodbye.

Efficient waste?

Plant those seeds
Those precious seeds
Fine tuned
Genetic purity

Sprinkle and tend them
Mix in those chemicals
To fend off those
Natural foes

Reap those rewards
With machines
Gobbling the ground
No resting
For the gentle or
Faint hearted

Work the weave
In the sweat shops
Paint the colours
Of the rainbow

Poisoned the rivers
Destroyed the workers
The aftermath
of the crop

Buy them
Discard them
Cram them
Sort them
Burn them - Waste not, want not?

Torment

Ok, the sea is ready to take another bashing.
Undercurrents hurling it against the rocks
No, no relief, out again and ready
Forced in, sprawling outwards.

It will continue to fight its plight
Knowing the moon will come
Save it from its torture
Resume it to a gentle ebb and flow
For a while before the new swell.

Thoughts

Your experience
Colours your world
And makes you see things
That may not be
As you think

Harmless gestures
Suddenly threats
Triggering reactions
In your body
Unrelated to this situation

These reactions
Seek to protect you
But wrap you up
In overreacting to
The world around you
Now.

Ceramic

The shiny white ceramic bowl
Has seen more sorts hover over its surface
Relieving themselves of badness
The brown exuded the same
Regardless of the source

Whether caviar or something scraped from rubbish
Whether jewelled or needle threaded veins
Innocent child or cantankerous witch
With rumpled folds of cloth, caught at the knees
We are all compromised, vulnerable and exposed

We are all human
Cleansed of filth
But evil thoughts and words
Are still trapped
In the tangles of our tissues.

Mail

All these lives
Hanging on strings
Above my bed

All those words
Painting pictures of
Their situations changed

All the years
Shared lives
Shared experiences

Happy Christmas.

Travel

The sound of this iron monster pulsating in my ears
As we speed towards the rocky highlands
All this journeying
Leaves the body tired
The mind, wasted and limp.

You

You are the one
With the bawling baby
With the crazy teenager
With the obligations

You are now the one
Exposed, left looking
Desperate, ignorant
No longer on the sidelines

You are the one
With the aching body
Decrepit and crumbling
Moaning for all
You are worth

You are the one
You criticized
Mocked, pitied
Not knowing
How it really felt
Now
You are the one.

Reserves

Wellingtons and shells
Material and letters
Energy and thoughts
Sorting the hoardings

Decisions and memories
Battling and sifting
Loneliness, excitement
For all things that matter.

Indecision

You think you've made your mind up
You hope it will turn out right
It's hard to know what's happening
When the destiny is out of sight

Your heart, head,
Body battling, aching
Never agreeing on a situation
No shattered illusions, no regret
Just a gentle desire
For peaceful contentment.

Escape

Racing words alighting the pen
Swamping the page with a deluge of frenzy
Emotions, expressions, news to send
Volcano exploding, firing this energy.

Out

Captured by the thought of getting away
Struggling to get on the road, to be free
Gypsy dancing with movements of frenzy
Gusts of action
The calmness
Begins to dwell.

Showers

Sprinkled from above
The simple joy as the sun peeks from behind the cloud
The sparkle shimmers through the dark and gloomy
shroud
Soggy oozing blanket of wetness
Mudbanks swelling
Puddles clouding
Hedges dripping
Rainwear seeping
Silk web glistening
Wellies sloshing
Soft patter of rain on the window
With the gentle breeze whispering to the branches
The air becomes fresh and sweet
Cut grass scent drifts and lingers there
Longer stalks waver in the new movement
The rainbows out
The showers complete.

Dust

We walk on the dust of the bones of our forefathers
If their bones were piled high
They'd reach to the sky
But still we do not talk of death

Death is our only certainty
No matter how well insured
No matter how fit or how hard we work
Our destiny is clear
but
We cannot mention it.

Lost hope

Here I am, emotionless face
No expression registering
Thoughts flying round the whirlpool of emotion
Beneath the thick curls and skull

Dynamite exploding inside me
Rage and sadness entwined
No scream to the outside world
They'll remain blind

Walls of self-consciousness engulf me
A twitch of a smile from this face
Cowering in and from myself
Resigning now to this solemn gaze

Walk these fields of dewy green
And feel the peace embalm me
The gentle fern breeze at my face
The smog and grease behind me

He doesn't care
Why should I bother?
I am not to be loved

Sighs of survival

Oppressive heat breaths endlessly on the suffocating
city
Gasping and choking fumes belching forth
Squinted eyes, strained faces, turned up noses
The stench of the Liffey
Exasperated sighs and sarcastic sorts

Seagulls wings tinged with grey
Hum of cars ceaselessly groans
Screeching brakes, road works thunder
Nerve shatter, hear the moans

Drenched city of smoggy droplets
Hazed beauty, chocked yet struggling
Eager bursts of sunshine
Silently suppressed.

Smothered

Like a butterfly trapped in loving hands
Struggling to be free
Smothered in hugs and kisses
Gasping for air
Gentle breeze from outside
Can't catch my wings.

Thorns

Sadly entwined in the thorns of life
Roses bloom, flourish, yet wither
Salt rubbed through in a wound ploughed deep
Mind is strong, yet heart's aquiver

Cold is the bite of the ice inside me
Expression torn just grimacing forth
Other joys blend, the bitter taste remains
Warmth is shown, acceptance is sought.

Feelings

Is there a feeling
I can have
That nobody else has known?

But maybe feelings
Are different for everyone
But we don't have
The words to express
The nuances?

Sort

The mind sifting through thoughts,
Unravelling knots but coming always to the same end
And around again

Happiness oozing from inside
Wells up
Overflows
And the empty cask remains.

Seizures of the sea

Keep your head high
When flowing against the tide
Like a seahorse
May the gentle sea caress and calm you
May your brain teem with life
Like the ocean.

Wild

Upsurging froth and foam from within
Raging limbs outstretch, draw back
Seizures, bellowing, madness in force
Saturated rocks sizzle in the wild wind

Roaring, screaming, crashing, howling
Darkness, whiteness, contrast then blend
Sharp freshness flings the eternal lash
Swallowed beauty unfolds again.

Blind

Deep inside this heart of mine torture is ingrained
The doors jammed ajar
Freedom is maimed
But a draught from outside escapes in

Resignation, enthusiasm
Mingled in one
Sights of the future
Rejecting the sun
Seen though the hazed glass
A reflection declined
Ways unexplainable
Leading the blind.

Touched

Magical music drifting on a gentle breeze
Shrouded in pink petals are the soft green leaves
Crunchy ground of beechnuts grown old
Such is the beauty nothing is cold

Eyes glancing over, peering then scampering
Wings in the branches fluttering when touching
Here, where the true music of all things blend
Peace all around, a gift he did send

When peace is shared, nothing is sought
Antagonistic dreams in the branches are caught
Roving hills of life's strange way
Entwining thoughts drifting fade away.

Caught off guard

This wild monster let loose
Enjoying its freedom
Races recklessly over the countryside
A gentle wisp of wind catches the daisy's head
nodding it gently
A neighbouring gasp pushes
This poor innocent stander-by
To the ground

This bad mannered monster bumps against the clouds
Causing them to sprawl forth in disarray
Such a bang he gave them
Their eyes well up with tears
Dark shadows creep across their original soft bright
faces
And they burst into floods of tears.

Scream

Why is she yapping?
Can't she see I'm going crazy?
The blaring music welling in my ear drums
They're going to burst
Stop, please

Don't bump off me - oh go away
No, there's nothing wrong
What's wrong with you?
Stop staring

My minds in a whirl, I hate everyone
I do, I do, I do – Well

Why can't I hibernate?
Can't I get out of here?

I want to scream
My teeth kept clenched
My eyes sink in the back of my head
My heart is being flung wildly around inside
It's twisted and torn
It's broken ripped apart
I'm trapped in my own vicious self
I cry out in desperation
What am I crying about?
I don't know. I don't care.

Up

Stretched limbs
Extended trunk
Upwards and out
In directed eagerness

Sprouted buds
Decaying leaves
Flourishing and nourishing
In cycles

Fineness of fingers
Strength of trunk
Beauty and fullness
In completeness
Of your stance.

Down

Majestic body lying
Broken in the grass
Scattered beauty
Not like seen last

Brutal force came
Ripped through this place
Skyline once filled
Now a bare grey space.

Circle of worry

Not long ago
We were the kids
The wild teenagers
Coming home
Late at night
Sneaking in
Hoping not to be caught

Now we stand here
Waiting for our own
To come through the door
Confront or relax?

Relief

Limbs aching in anticipation
Mind lulling in hope
Senses dulling and awakening
One touch and sleep sinks in warmth.

Anticipation

Life in my mind
Sounds in my ears
Flushed my face
Eagerness, no fears

Collapsing my legs
Racing my heart
Wide my eyes
Ready to start.

Crossroads

Thoughts colliding
Truth unveiled
Hidden crust crumbles
All attempts fail
To quench the suggestion of new ways

The time is now
Grasp or fall
It will pass
No recall

Change or stay the same.

Meeting

My feet brought me such a long way
My mind came trailing behind
It met my feet
Short discussion pursued
Then they were on their way again.

Word perfect

Storming the system
Sifting the returns
Poised to capture
The perfect form

Energy fading
Brain cells clicking
Hunger for one thing
Words

Subconscious open
Open and leaking
Words of unexpected flux

Fleeing their dark cells
Seizing the paper
Predestined
No reflux

Resulting forms remaining
Waiting for interpretation
Lie in anticipated trust.

Yes

Bursting with excitement
Exploding inside
Scream in my brain
Heart open wide

Laughter with hilarity
Giggling inside
Ease in my movements
Smile beaming wide.

Look at me

Don't pull me behind you bicycle
With gravel in my knees
Don't leave me here grovelling
With no view of the trees

Lift my head
Look at my face
See my eyes
Forlorn in this place.

Visitor

I touch your face
With the gentlest massage
Warm and caressing
You breathing me in

Breathing in memories
Of the scents I carry
From other places
And time since lost

But your delight
Was another's sorrow
As I lashed their homes
Into the sea

As I caused havoc
Uprooting trees and
Wrecking families
With my wild thrusts

I am a moody thing.

Driver

Push over
Let me drive
My own car
I've my feet on the pedals
Give me the wheel

Drive your own car
Or be a passenger for a while.

Independent?

Struggling together
Makes it better
Regardless of the age
The century
The problems

Struggling alone
Thinking you're the only one
Private and free
But alone.

Sweet Naivety

Destiny or madness
Drawn by the fun
Lured by the mystery
Of waters unknown

Surface untouched
Unrippled so clear
Murky water lurking
Waiting so near

Mirror Mirror

The mirror returns
The requested view
The altered perception
Of the person true

The other seen
Though changing each day
Remains to the viewer
A stable image of the brain

Dreams, understandings
Fears, misconceptions
Create and destroy
Visions of happiness.

Forgive

Why worry
How significant is your problem
In the larger scale of things
Is it life threatening?
Will you land on the street?

Let's keep things
In perspective
Nobody is going to die
Because of you
Stupid mistake.

Missed summer

The air changed bringing new warmth
Easing the tension
On cold skin taut

The feeling remained
Undisturbed by this touch
Buried in the rubble
Wasted and lost

Greed

Smelling of boardroom
Wrinkled children in suits
Deciding the future of others
Flick of a pen, nod agreed
A greed replacing need

Wrinkled children in suits
Passed from nappies to here
Buried the need for
Something more
Something more than suits

Yearning the smell of boardrooms
Substituting fears for breeze
Airs of confidence, measured words
Concealing their true needs.

War

I inherited your thoughts
I inherited your words
What is left for me?

The stale taste of bitterness
The churning within
The sharp sting of your ideals

Regardless of cause
People are fought
Maimed and slaughtered
With undigested thoughts.

Trust

Thousands have tried to find
The meaning of life
Does the earth ever question
Its existence?

It follows its path
Into the unknown
Trusting it won't
Collide, with all those
Flying objects

Can we do the same?

I can't take

I can't take
Another day of washing
I'd rather stay in bed
My legs like stumps
They dangle there
My spirit is long dead

I drag myself
From day to day
From crutches to wheelchair
Drag from work to
Home again
No one notices
When I'm there

Some say I'm cranky
No love of life
Some say I have no cheer
I wish them my wheelchair
My life
A constant effort
Year after year.

Graveside wars

Did you ever notice
The competition
At the graveside?
It only starts there
But afterwards
It's worse

Never are so many
People fighting for
One person's attention
That they will never
Receive again

So many aspects
Of one person's life
All turning up and
Confronting each other
On one day

Friends, lovers, family
Loved, rejected, bitter
Sad, heartbroken, glad
So many years, months
Days, moments
Of one's life
Standing side by side

The closeness, the last times
The coincidences, the stories never told
The thoughts in each head
The wonder of the immediate family
Who are all these people?

How can there be so many
Surely they don't feel as I do?

Maybe they do
Each life
Each death
Touches so many others

Inevitable

We never talk of life
Till the end is
In our field of vision
Talk about what's important
Think about
What is worth
The effort

The effort of staying alive
Keeping healthy and happy
The effort of paddling
Often without
Direction

Just keeping a roof
Over our heads
Keeping food on the table
Keeping worry at bay

Worry gnaws at our substance
Dissolves our insides with its acid
Worms its way
To the heart
Of our lives

Our lives are for living
Our time is our own
We need to look at
The way we have grown

What do we want?

Close

Being with you
Helps me see things clearer
Takes me out of my head
You ask the right questions
We philosophise and laugh
Laugh at ourselves

Talking to you
Rises me up
I shake off the dirt
That has been pulling me down
We tease and untangle
Our cobwebs, our chains
We set ourselves free
Till we talk again

Eating with you
Makes me taste everything
Be present and see
How good
I have it
Having you
With me.

Message

The written word
Seeped from a mind
Unrelated to your own
But transforming your world
With each phrase
Eases your burden
Increases your fears
Allows you to wallow
In your hidden thoughts
Brings to the surface
Memories forgotten
Fears dug deep
Gives understanding
Or wrenches you to
Another level of consciousness
The written word never
Leaves you unchanged
Never has a voice
Such an attentive audience.

Impression

Once spoken
It cannot be recalled
Once heard
It cannot be erased
Once seen
It's locked behind your eyes
Once felt,
The imprint remains.

Live

You could stay in the ground
Bury your head
And never risk
Moving in any direction

You could be just fine
Safe and quiet

Or you could burst forth
See the sun
Get lashed by the rain
Grow you leaves
And lose them

Feel, what's the sense?
And grow despite yourself.
It won't be all easy,
But the beautiful moments
Will make it worthwhile

LIVE IT

.

Savour

After the rain clears
And the black clouds break up
In the sun
I drink the fresh soil
Savour the wet leaves
In my nose
And ease into a new feeling
Everything gentler now
Harsh edges cleared
Nothing shrill or nerve wrecking
I know I'll find my way.

Spin

It's amazing to think
Of all us people
Rushing around
When the world is spinning
Not only around and around
But in the immense nothingness
Its path known only to itself

We run here and there
With such importance

The sniper

The sniper is ready
Loaded full
Fuelled on bitterness
Never expressed

Her mouth was pursed
Her eyes cold hard
The valve was closed
But not for long

It could have dribbled
But the force was great
The fury couldn't subside
Once instigated

It flooded and destroyed
The victim in place
Shook and rocked
Till the silence struck

What could she do?
She knew she was wrong
Her victim wounded
Her bitterness too strong

Messages could have been left
Warnings given
The fear was too great
So everything was hidden

Hidden and buried
But never deep enough
The bitterness rose
And killed all love

Observed

Expressions of strangers
I don't know
Telling me more of themselves
Than those I know

Idleness perfect for
Registering thoughts on
Faces unaware of
Being observed

Tune

If the strings are pulled tighter
They will snap
They are my strings
My noise
My tightness

Let go, let loose
Unwind
They say
But not completely
I want to play
The song
Of my life
Perfectly tuned.

Question

My thoughts are borrowed from another
My emotions are not
I may look like my mother
But that's not my lot

A sticky hedgehog
Collecting as I go
Letting go is not easy
But it's what I need
To grow

Growing to another form
With each passing day
Sifting and sorting
So I can find my way.

Knowing

I thought I knew you
I really did
Maybe it was
Part of me
I thought
I knew me too

Shocking really
To realize
You're not what you thought
You were
Or what anybody else could have
Dreamed of either.

Death

Death presents us with our life
Serves us our regrets and joys
On a platter

It doesn't care what we've achieved
It will take us anyway
It pulls us in
Whether we are
Willing or not

It is inevitable
What choice do we have?
To live our lives
When we have it.

Hidden

The girls with the spots and glasses
May be great in bed
The beauty queen glowing and smiling
May be rotting inside with fear
The businessman controlled and ice cold
May be wishing he was wearing a nappy
The brat who is acting up
May want a hug
And not a smack

We hide in our bodies
As best we can
But as we age
Our organs complain
With all
They've been forced to hold
Under the skin
Under control.

Control

Hiding beneath the dashboard
Afraid to look ahead
I keep my muscles taunt
One foot on the gas
The other braking at any
Sense of danger

I lie here exhausted
Worrying and reacting
Fumbling in the dark
I must lift myself
Out of here

Raise my head from the dark
Look life in the eye
And decide
To hold onto the steering wheel
Aim for something and
Change direction
At will.

Trapped

I was trapped
Trapped in my head
My body grasping
At a thought
But letting it go
Not knowing
Not knowing what I
Could say

How could I express
What's running though my veins
My need
My need to feel
Extreme feelings
Indulge rather than
Express.

Left

He left
He just turned around and left
No choice given
His mind made up
I stand here numb
Sad and mad

How could he do it?
Never indicate
Never give me a chance
Never think
What we had built
Was worth
Anything

He's broken my heart
My trust, my hope
He's everybody's hero
Now condemned

The criticism gives
Me some comfort
But not enough
To ease the pain.

Guilt

Guilt written all
Over me
Guilt of the first degree
Never enough
Or always too much
I'm pulled by
What way
To be

All I want is to
Live life to the full
Live life and
Not let you down
Feeling loved and involved
Struggling to
Pull away

Tied in knots

I'm the boat going nowhere
Tied to the harbour wall
The wall
That gave me
Protection
Smashing me now
As the storm whips
And lashes out

Fear has held me here
Tied me up in knots
Theres nothing boat like about me
Just bobbing up and down

If I'd never felt the rush
Of the ocean
Never wondered at the
Ocean deep
I wouldn't know what
I'm missing
But I do
Everyday
Making me weep

I'm soaked in your emotion
Soaked and drowned
To the skin and
Within.

Addict

Do what you feel
They say
How can I do that?
When I feel desire
Guilt, thrill, fear
Pulling me in all directions

What steers my life
In the end
My logic, good sense
Or the chemicals rushing
Though my blood stream

You can call me what
You want
Abuse won't get us
Anywhere
We're all human
Steered by the
Strongest chemical.

Consumed

My affections for you are misplaced
Thoughts of you have found a crevice
And taken seed
Dominating my waking hours and
My dreams
There is no sense in asking why
You permeate my being
Soaking every moment
Causing me to forget
Important tasks
My dearest ones.

Stony path

The strongest tree
Has leaves that have
Stretched to the sun
And roots that have explored
The deepest darkness
Of the soil

Out of the darkest of soils
Come the brightest of colours

The strongest wisest man
Knows his potential
For goodness and bad
Depending on the circumstances

There is no wave without a crest and a trough
Surf

Nano Nano

Since we've discovered the nanosecond
We divided our lives
Much more
Time is money
Make use of each moment
Make use of each nanosecond

Where do we store these nano-experiences?
Stuff them all
Into our bodies
Wonder why we can't think straight
Our bodies twitching and recording.

Sense

What does it matter, what we know?
The deals, the decisions we've made
The gadgets we have
The speed we travel
What does it matter at all?

Tact time

All the clocks in the world
Ticking,
At the same time
All the people watching them
Ticking
Rushing, waiting

Watching the clock

Holidays

When the sun shines
When the clock is not
Demanding attention
When love has time
When smiles turns to chats
When hugs last much longer

The clock puts an end to that.

Dance

The vibration pulses within me
I can't sit here and not move
It shakes my body
Wakes my shy self
Swings me round
Making me laugh
Making me real
I float round that hall and feel new life

Memories race to my eyes
I smile, I see them all
Friends called up
Places, hidden return
I want to live it again

I live it new
New body
New people
Old music

Celebrate

Northwest wind

The rain on the caravan roof as I sleep
Pitter, patter reaches monumental levels
When the northwest wind rushes round that mountain
foot and shakes us
The initial shock ebbs and the shaking in my stomach
subsides and I lull into sleep
Brightness floods through the tattered curtains and the
seagull makes his way across our roof
We wake and laugh as we hear him jump and trot
sounding like a herd of elephants

Daydreaming in the city bustling and bursting at the
seams
I hear the seagull cry and laugh and wake me again
Make me realise I am living on an island
Floating slowly away from the mainland
The sharp saltiness in my nose and skin and hair
Keeping me Irish

And what am I doing here standing on the side of the
lake in Zürich
The gulls don't cry and laugh here to the same extent
But the sharp northwest wind blows
The clearness in the sky
The light lifting me
As I feel a new beginning
A merging of Swiss and Irish life
The Alps covered in snow
The Irish wind meeting them and
Dropping their load.

Missing

The sun is not shining
But I'm warm in my heart
Your hands not beside me
But I don't feel far apart

I'm waiting to see you
To feel you close
Surrounded by old friends
But I think of you most

Miles I have travelled
Hasn't changed the feelings inside
I need you, I love you
My man, wild child.

Creation

We made a little human
She came into the world today
See her wiggle
Hear her scream
She grows
She smiles
She brings us joy

A person, little girl,
No, not a toy
We're tired, so tired
Can we go on?
So lovely, so nice
But not all fun
Feed, next feed
And nappy change
Her little cry
Her tummy pains.

Smothering

Let him go
Let him free
You don't need to know
Where he's going
Who he's seen

If he loves you
He'll return
If not, holding on to him
Won't make his love burn
His love can't be
Just totally for me
He needs to be wanted
Needs to be free

I need to feel peace
Contentment in my heart
What do I need
For this to start?

If I hold him too close
I'll smother his love
Let him too free
I won't see him enough

A balance is needed
For love to grow
Release my worrying thoughts
Let myself flow.

Crystals

He once flew by on his bicycle
Onlookers cowering from the speed
She once charmed that young chap
With her laughter and wit

What impure deed
Caused the bright crystals
To fall as deep sediment
Choking all hopes of freedom
Freedom from bitterness

Mystery

Waves on my stomach kicking from within
Jumping and twirling
Just beneath my skin

Sprouting

Flower grows out of stone wall
Theres something growing in me
Can it survive the heaving, the uproar
Riveting through my body

Morning and night
Joy, frustration
Depression and loneliness
Torn apart inside and out
It's not a sickness!
I've never been so sick
It'll pass
When?
I want to shout

Food my friend, my enemy in one
Eat, get sick, repeat again
Nobody said this would be
No evidence of this, I could see

A flicker of hope, with thoughts of a child
The pictures are distorted with my feelings inside
I try to do my best, it's not enough
I try to rest, to feel some love

The battle goes on
When does it end?
Sometimes relieved by close ones and friends
I'm in stagnant water with no hope of a rush
Hormones settle down give my spirit a push up.

Anger

The terrible heat rising in me
Flooding my brain
Dulling my senses till
I'm not sane

Let it out
Hold it back
Scream
Be quiet
Conflicting battles
On the same track
Frustration

Thoughts flying around
Long sleepless nights
Tossing and turning
Losing this fight
D anger

Home

I wanted to know
You were here
Feel your soft embrace

To know I could come back
To be with you
Nothing has filled your space.

Hero?

I'm a boy
Grown into a man
You want a hero
I don't think
That I can.

You want me to know
How you're feeling inside
How can I feel that?
When my feelings
I hide

You want a guardian
How should I be that?
I'm only a boy
Grown into a man.

Beautiful

Why all that perfume?
When you can wear a smile for free
That look
That perfect style
Doesn't really do it for me.

Connected

If every drop of water never leaves our planet
If every atom circulates beneath our celestial sky
If every breathe of air moving
Leaves you and enters me
We are all connected
More connected
Than I ever thought
Could be.